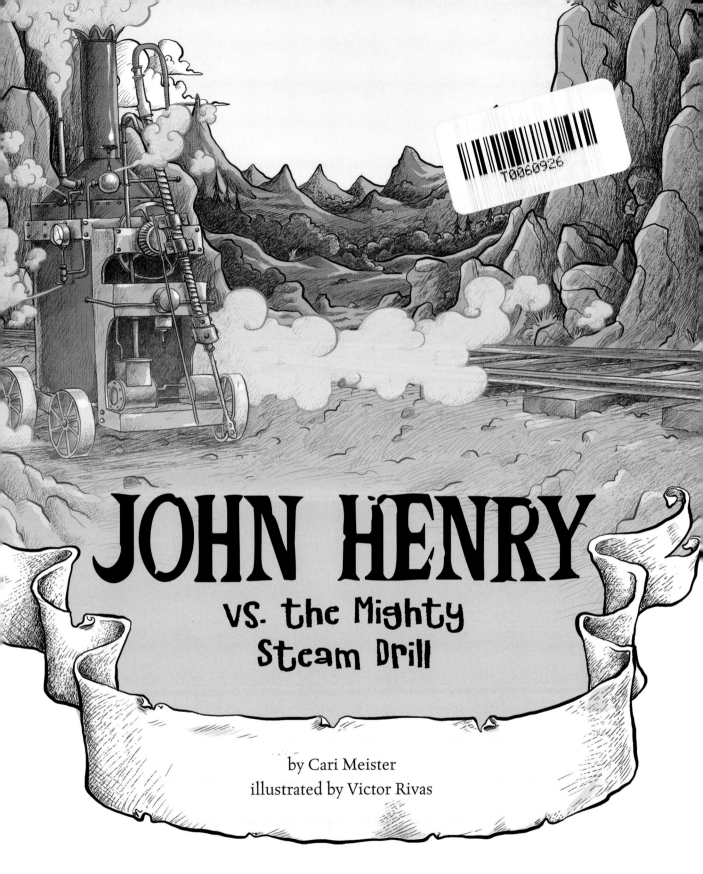

JOHN HENRY
vs. the Mighty Steam Drill

by Cari Meister
illustrated by Victor Rivas

PICTURE WINDOW BOOKS
a capstone imprint

JOHN HENRY–
Was He Real?

Back in the days before cars and jet airplanes, there was the railroad. It took thousands of strong men to build the railroad across the United States. But one steel-drivin' man stands above the rest—John Henry.

People disagree about whether or not the John Henry of legend was real. We do know that building railroads was difficult, rhythmic work. Because of this the men often sang. Songs helped the men keep the pace of their work. The legendary John Henry was the subject of many of the songs.

Eventually steam drills were introduced to the railroad companies. The men who had built the steam drills thought the machines could work faster than any man. On at least one occasion—sometime in the 1870s—they decided to see if the steam drill WAS better than a man. Who was tested against the machine? Legend states that it was John Henry.

The night John Henry was born, the skies turned black and rumbled. In fact, the very moment John Henry took his first breath, a bolt of lightnin' struck a giant sycamore tree.

Oh Lordy, was John Henry a mighty fine babe! His legs were the size of tree trunks. And his arms—they were as long as the kitchen table. But most surprisin' of all was what he clutched in his newborn baby hand—a 10-pound steel-drivin' hammer!

Yessiree, John Henry used that hammer.

BANG! He built a fort when he was just 3 years old!

CLANG! At the age of 6, John Henry built a road!

CLANK! By the time he was 9 years old, he carved

a statue from a mountain!

John was always singin' while he was hammerin' away:

I was born with a hammer in my hand, oh, yeah.

I was born with a hammer in my hand.

Got me a hammer in my hand, yes, sir.

Got me a fine hammer in my hand.

When John Henry turned 14, he said to his daddy, "I heard they be needin' some good strong men to work on the railroad. I reckon they could use my help, yes, sir. I reckon they could use my help."

So his mama cooked up a fine farewell feast. When he was as stuffed as a turkey on Thanksgivin' Day, John Henry set off to find the railroad camp.

Well, John hadn't gotten too far when he heard all kinds of screamin' and shoutin.' A hospital was burnin' down, and people were trapped inside!

Faster than a jackrabbit, John Henry used his hammer to pound through them walls. He carried out every man, woman, and child.

As John Henry continued on his way, he felt obliged to help others.

BING! He built 243 homes for the poor!

BANG! He saved people from a terrible rockslide!

CLANG! He built a bridge across the Alleghany River!

All the while John was singin' away:

> *I was born with a hammer in my hand, oh, yeah.*
> *I was born with a hammer in my hand.*
> *Got me a hammer in my hand, yes, sir.*
> *Got me a fine hammer in my hand.*

Finally John Henry saw it—the C & O Railroad work camp. He heard bangin' and clangin' and workers singin'. His skin started to prickle, for he knew this was the life for him.

He rushed over to the captain. "My name's John Henry, sir, and I'm a steel-drivin' man," he said. "No hammer on this good ol' earth rings like mine, no sir. No hammer rings quite like mine."

Captain Tommy smiled as wide as my granny's bottom and said,
"Use that hammer of yours, my son. Drive those stakes into rock."

John Henry drove those steel stakes into the mountain, day after day, year after year. He did more work in one day than other men did in a week. He worked so fast that his hammer caught fire several times a day!

Of course, he was always smilin' and singin' too.

My name is John Henry,
and I'm a steel-drivin' man.
Got me a hammer in my hand, oh, yeah.
Got me a fine hammer in my hand.

One day a man from the C & O approached Captain Tommy.
"This here steam drill can drive holes into rock quick as lightnin',"
he said. "This machine will do the work of 100 men!"

The workers looked mighty worried. Where would they find work if the machine took away their jobs?

The men looked at John Henry, and John Henry knew just what to do.

"Now don't you worry, friends," John said. "Don't you worry a bit. Before that steam drill will beat me down, I'll die with a hammer in my hand, oh, yeah. I'll die with a hammer in my hand."

John turned to the man and said, "I've got a deal for you, yes, sir. I've got a deal for you."

That man listened to John's proposition real good. And this is how it went: If John Henry could clear more rock than that steam drill in one day, then the man and his machine would turn tail and head home.

The next mornin' John was polishin' up his 20-pound hammer. The railroad man oiled his machine.

The crowd gathered. And when that startin' shot fired,
John Henry jumped to the top of the mountain. The railroad
man started the steam drill.

All day John Henry kept hammerin' away and fillin' his holes with dynamite.

BING! BANG! CLANG!

The steam drill was workin' away too.

WHIZ ... HISS ... CLINK ...

But no one could tell who was winnin'.

As the sun set, the finishin' shot rang out. John came down from the top of that mountain. The railroad man stopped the hissin' machine.

The captain got out his tape measure. "John Henry sunk a 14-foot hole," he yelled, "and the steam drill's is only 9-feet deep!"

The workers cheered, but John Henry was worn out. He fell down, clutchin' his hammer to his chest.

Captain Tommy held John Henry's head and looked into his eyes. "That was a mighty fine job you did, John Henry."

"I've beat him, Cap'n Tommy. I've beat him to the bottom, but I'm dead." John Henry kissed his hammer, groaned, and closed his eyes.

Some folks say John Henry is buried in the sand not too far from that tunnel. And any time a train rumbles by the spot, passengers salute that steel-drivin' man, yes, sir. They praise John Henry—the steel-drivin' man.

The legend of John Henry spread across the United States over time through songs. As workers traveled across the country, their songs changed. The songs took on new flavors—the flavors of the people singing them. Some people added that John Henry had a wife. Some people added that he had a baby. When people sang about John Henry's death, some claimed he had a heart attack. Others said that a blood vessel had broken in his head. There are many versions of the John Henry legend, both in song and story.

John Henry's can-do attitude has been championed for more than 100 years.

First railroad workers sang the story. Then musicians, playwrights, and storytellers began telling it. John Henry's legend lives on today because it is a tale of hard work and perseverance. John Henry's legend proves that one person can make a difference in the lives of many.

Learn More About Folktales

Although there are many different American folktales, each story contains similar pieces. Take a look at what usually makes up an American folktale:

hero—the main character of an American folktale is most often a hero with exaggerated abilities, or abilities that seem greater than they actually are

humor—most early American folktales are funny; the exaggerated characters and situations add to the humor

hyperbole—exaggeration; used in folktales to make the characters seem larger than life, almost magical

quest—a challenge; most early American folktales include a challenge that the main character faces; the challenge may include defeating a villain

slang—words and phrases that are more often used in speech, and are usually used by a certain group of people; common cowboy slang consisted of words and sayings such as "There's no use beatin' the devil around the stump," which meant there's no use avoiding a difficult task

Critical Thinking Using the Common Core

1. American folktales often include hyperbole, or exaggeration. Can you find some examples of hyperbole in this story? (Key Ideas and Details)

2. If you could retell a story from your past, what details would you include and why? Which common folktale elements could you use to make the story even more exciting? (Integration of Knowledge and Ideas)

Glossary

blood vessel—a narrow tube that carries blood through the body

champion—to support the cause of

folktale—a traditional, timeless tale people enjoy telling

legend—a story handed down from earlier times; legends may be based on facts, but they are not entirely true

obliged—to feel a need to act on something

perseverance—the act of continually trying or working toward a goal or belief

proposition—a plan, deal, or proposal

salute—to give a sign of respect or recognition to someone, especially when someone is coming or going

Read More

Lester, Julius. *John Henry*. New York: Dial Books, 1994.

Nelson, Scott Reynolds, with Marc Aronson. *Ain't Nothing But a Man: My Quest to Find the Real John Henry*. Washington, D.C.: National Geographic, 2008.

Peters, Stephanie True, retold by. *John Henry, Hammerin' Hero*. Graphic Spin. Mankato, Minn.: Stone Arch Books, 2010.

Thanks to our advisers for their expertise, research, and advice:

Elizabeth Tucker Gould, Professor of English
Binghamton University

Terry Flaherty, PhD, Professor of English
Minnesota State University, Mankato

Editor: Shelly Lyons
Designer: Tracy Davies McCabe
Art Director: Nathan Gassman
Production Specialist: Jennifer Walker
The illustrations in this book were created with pen and ink with watercolor wash.

Design element: Shutterstock: 06photo

Picture Window Books are published by Capstone,
1710 Roe Crest Drive, North Mankato, Minnesota 56003
www.capstonepub.com

Library of Congress Cataloging-in-Publication Data
Meister, Cari.
John Henry vs. the mighty steam drill / by Cari Meister.
pages cm. — (Picture window books. American folk legends)
ISBN 978-1-4795-5430-0 (library binding)
ISBN 978-1-4795-5447-8 (paperback)
ISBN 978-1-4795-5455-3 (eBook PDF)
1. John Henry (Legendary character)—Legends. I. Title.
II. Title: John Henry versus the mighty steam drill.
PZ8.1.M498Joh 2015
398.2—dc23   2014001531

Printed in the United States of America
in North Mankato, MN.
032014   008087CGF14

Internet Sites

FactHound offers a safe, fun way to find Internet sites related to this book. All of the sites on FactHound have been researched by our staff.

Here's all you do:

Visit *www.facthound.com*

Type in this code: 9781479554300

Check out projects, games and lots more at
www.capstonekids.com

Look for all the books in the series:

Davy Crockett and the Great Mississippi Snag
John Henry vs. the Mighty Steam Drill
Johnny Appleseed Plants Trees Across the Land
Pecos Bill Tames a Colossal Cyclone